STREET ACTION

Contents

STREET GAMES

Street games
have been played
for a long time.

To be
a street game player
you have to have:

- friends,

- a street,

- and a game!

MARBLES

Long ago,
people played marbles
with nuts and little stones.

They played
games of marbles
in the streets.

Today,
marble players
still play marbles
in the street.

Try this Mighty Marble Game!

- Draw a circle.

- Get the players to put five or six of their marbles in the circle.

- Take turns, hitting the marbles out of the circle.
  If you hit a marble out, you get a point!
  Your marble must stay in the circle.

- If you hit a marble out take another turn.
  Go from where your marble stopped.

But look out!
Marble players
can keep your marbles.
They can keep the marbles
that they hit out of the circle!

Play safe!
Don't play marbles on the street!

5

STREET HOCKEY

People say
a kind of street hockey was played
by the Wichita Native Americans.
The Wichita Native Americans
tell of a game that they played
with balls and clubs
made from bone.

Today, people play street hockey
on dead-end streets.

You need:
- two teams,
- five to eight players for each team,
- boxes or buckets for a goal,
- a hockey stick.

If you don't have a hockey stick,
a broom will do.

How to play street hockey
- Start from the middle of the court.
- Hit the ball with the stick.
- Do not swing the stick up
  when you hit the ball.
- Get the ball
  past the other team
  into the goal.

Play safe!
Keep your hockey
stick low!

Be cool!

HANDBALL

Handball has been played
for a long, long time
in lots of places in the world.
Handball is good to play.

All you need is:
- a wall,
- a court,
- a ball.

Play safe!
Watch the ball
all the time!

How to play handball
- Player One hits the ball
  onto the wall.
- The ball goes in Player Two's court
  with one bounce.
- Player Two hits the ball
  back onto the wall.
- The ball goes in Player One's court
  with one bounce.

You lose a turn if you:
- let the ball bounce
  more than once in your court,
- hit a line with the ball,
- cannot hit the ball back.

BASKETBALL

Basketball
is a good street game.
You can shoot baskets
with your friends.
You can bounce the ball
past your friends
and shoot a goal.
But look out! Your friends
will get the ball from you
and shoot goals, too!

Play safe!
Always shoot
baskets with
your friends.
Don't go alone!

The basket in this game
has a beeper.
The beeper tells people
who cannot see
where the basket is.

HACKEY SACK

Hackey sack is a street game.
One player or a lot of players
can play hackey sack.
Hackey sack players
must keep the hackey sack
up in the air.
The hackey sack
cannot hit the ground.

How to play hackey sack

Keep the hackey sack
up in the air
- with your feet,
- with your knees,
- with your chest,
- with your head.

You cannot keep the hackey sack
up in the air
with your hands.

Play safe!
Watch the
players. Don't
smash into them!

Street Skating

Play safe! Always wear safety gear!

Skateboarder Talk

A **goofyfoot** is a move.
The skater rides
with the right foot forward.

A **backside** is a move.
The skater turns the board
in the same way
that the toes point.

An **ollie** is a move.
The skater
lifts the board
off the ground.
No hands touch
the board.

A **wheelie** is a trick.
The skater skates
on one set of wheels only.

A **kickturn**
is a move.
The skater
turns the board
by stepping
on the tail.
The front wheels
are lifted off
the ground.

A **slam** is a crash.

A **bail** is a crash
that is planned.

15

In-line Skating

In-line skaters skate on the city streets, too.
In-line skaters stroke and glide.
They know how to fall.
They know how to skate.
They know how to go fast!

Play safe!
Look out for
children and
old people!

In-line skaters learn how to fall.
Now, they can learn
extreme skating stunts and tricks!

Skateboard Stunts

Written by
James Alcock-Roberts

I just got my new skateboard. Wow!
It has great trucks and wheels and bearings.
I called up my friend.
I told him about my new skateboard.
He came over and we started skating.
We went to a dead-end street.
There was a box in the street.
I could ollie over the box.
An ollie is a board jump.

I tried a 50-50.
To do a 50-50 both trucks
must scrape down the wall.
I could do it on a little wall,
But the thing is I could do it!

My friend and I
went to the bowl at the park.
There were two more people there, too.
They did 180s and 180 power slides.
A power slide is when you flick the board
so that the back wheels go sideways
and make a screeching noise.

19

There are lots of walls by my house.
I can do nose slides on the walls.
A nose slide is when you slide
down a wall on the nose of the board.
It is better if you wax the wall.

My friend tried to do a trick.
It is called a kick flip.
A kick flip is when you do an ollie
but the board spins around
up in the air.

A boy was doing kick flips
and ollie to manual.
Now an ollie to manual is an ollie
that lands on the two back wheels.
We tried our kick flips in the rain,
and my kick flip landed in a puddle.
I was wet!

Happy skating!

James

S.P.U.D. – YOU'RE OUT!

Written by Sharon Capobianco
Illustrated by Mrinal Mitra

Today I played a new game.
I played it with my aunt,
and with my grandma and grandpa.

Josh and Sal played, too.
Josh's grandma and grandpa came.
They played, too.
Sal's dad and Uncle Kent came.
They played, too.

My grandma said the game was Spud.
Grandma gave us all a number.
I was number **three.**

Play safe!
Play games in
the park – not
on the street!

Sal's dad was **it.** He had the ball. He threw the ball up in the air. He called out number **seven.** He ran away.

I ran away.

I was not number **seven.**

My aunt ran away.

She was not number **7.**

The grandmas and grandpas ran away.

They were not number **seven.**

Uncle Kent did not run away.
He was number **seven**.
Uncle Kent ran after the ball.
Uncle Kent got the ball.
Uncle Kent called out **Spud.**

When Uncle Kent called out **Spud,**
we all stopped.

Uncle Kent looked at all of us.
He looked to see where to throw the ball.
He threw the ball at Josh's grandma.
The ball hit Josh's grandma.
Josh's grandma got an **S.**
She was **it.**

Josh's grandma threw the ball up in the air.
She called out number **three.**
She ran away.

My aunt and
Sal's dad ran
away.

Josh and his grandma
ran away.

26

The grandpas ran away.

Sal ran away.

I ran to get the ball. I called out **SPUD.**

27

I looked to see where to throw the ball.

I threw the ball at Sal.

Sal got away.

I got an S like Josh's grandma.

I was it again.

I threw the ball up in the air.

I called out number four.

I ran away.

I tripped.

I fell over.

Play safe!
Watch where
you are running!

Josh got the ball and called out **Spud.**

I knew Josh would throw the ball at me.

He did. It hit me. Now I had **SP.**

Two more times, and I would be out of the game.

I got up. I was **it** again.
This time, I threw the ball up high.
I called out number **six.**
We played and played the game.
In the end, the first one out
was my grandpa.

He got hit by the ball four times.
He had **SPUD!**
After Grandpa got out,
I got hit by the ball two more times.
So I was out, too.

Which street games do you like the best?

Then Josh got out and Uncle Kent. Then Grandma said, "That's it! We are all tired out!"

And we were.

Glossary

🐾 **baskets** – the netted hoops through which players shoot their basketballs to score goals

🐾 **bearings** (of a skateboard) – the parts under the board on which the skateboard wheels turn

🐾 **bowl** (skateboard) – a basinlike hole in the ground that skateboarders use to try out their moves and tricks

🐾 **dead-end street** – a street that is closed off at one end

🐾 **extreme skating** – a way of skating that includes tricks or stunts, such as jumping off ramps and riding stairs

🐾 **marbles** – a game of skill played with small balls (called marbles)

🐾 **trucks** – the part of a skateboard that fixes the wheels to the board